Written by Fiona Waters

Illustrated by Ken Oliver

ACKNOWLEDGEMENTS
The publisher would like to thank the following for their kind permission to reproduce their photographs:

a = above; b = below; c = centre; l = left; r = right; t = top.

Ancient Art and Architecture Collection: 2 cr;
Barnabys Picture Library: 28 bl; **J. Allan Cash Ltd:** 29 tr;
Colorsport: 16 bl; **C.M. Dixon:** 3 tr; **Photostage:** Donald Cooper 11 bl, 12 cr; **Planet Earth Pictures:** Scott McKinley 10 cl;
Redferns Music Picture Library: Henrietta Butler 19 cl;
David Redfern 36 b; **Rex Features:** 39 t; John Gooch 26 bl;
Peter Sanders Photography: 18 bl;

A Funfax Book
Copyright © 1998 Funfax Ltd,
Woodbridge, Suffolk, IP12 1AN, England.
All rights reserved.

BEGINNERS, PLEASE

The earliest musical notes were probably made by prehistoric people calling to each other over the plains, or singing around fires in celebration after a successful hunting expedition.

Toe Tapping

As far back as 40,000 BC, people were using instruments to make sounds. Reindeer toe bones had a hole drilled in them to make a single note for signalling. The earliest musical instrument to have survived to the present day is an eleven-string harp found in the Royal Tombs at Ur, in modern Iraq.

Tut's Trumpet

The Ancient Egyptians played music at their feasts and in their ceremonies. Pictures of musical instruments were painted on the walls in the tomb of Pharaoh Tutankhamun (around 1360-1350 BC), and a kind of trumpet was found.

Ancient Egyptian flautist

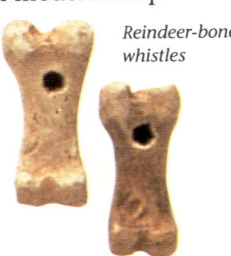

Reindeer-bone whistles

Heavenly Voices

Music began to play an important part in religious ceremonies around 950 BC. According to the Bible, when King Solomon's temple was dedicated in Jerusalem, one hundred and twenty priests played trumpets, while others played harps and cymbals.

It's All Greek

The Greeks were the first people to write down music, using letters from their alphabet. Many of the words we use today, such as 'orchestra' and 'harmony', come from Greek. The word 'music' itself comes from the Greek word 'mousike', meaning the arts of dance, music and poetry.

Greek painting

When in Rome

The Romans played music during games in the Colosseum – the great amphitheatre in Rome where gladiators fought to the death. At one performance there were one hundred trumpets, one hundred horns and two hundred pipes. What a blast!

The Colosseum, Rome

MEDIEVAL MUSIC 1000-1599

In the early Middle Ages, church music was based on ancient Jewish chanting with no accompanying instruments. Then composers put together more complex part singing, where a second, third, or even fourth melody was added to the basic tune.

Doh, a Deer...

An Italian monk called Guido d'Arezzo (around 900-1050) came up with the first proper system of writing music down. He devised the *staff* (otherwise known as the *stave*) and named all the notes, to help singers:

doh, ray, me, fah, soh, lah, te, doh.

Travelling Tunes

Poets and musicians called troubadours travelled from village to village singing songs about courtly love and chivalry. They were very romantic figures. If you look at paintings of this time you will see what they looked like. Troubadours would gather for public festivals or weddings, and their tunes and melodies spread across Europe.

Keeping Up Appearances

Before long, kings, nobles, abbots, even towns began to have their own groups of musicians who provided entertainment on special occasions. These bands would play instrumental versions of the troubadours' vocal tunes.

Next Page, Please

The first complete piece of music was printed in 1473. Before then, it had to be copied out by hand – a very long and slow process! Once music sheets were printed and available, the demand for simple music for amateur players increased. The first popular (or *pop*) music was born!

Massed Choirs

While popular music became much simpler, church music became more complex, as composers tried to express their deep religious beliefs. One of the most famous pieces of this time is a *motet* (a piece of music for unaccompanied voices) by an Englishman called Thomas Tallis (around 1505-1585). It is written in forty separate parts, for eight choirs. Imagine losing your place in the middle of that!

BAROQUE MUSIC 1600-1749

The first ever public opera house opened in Venice, in 1637. An opera is a bit like a play, but the performers sing as well as act. The earliest operas involved a lot of speaking, called *recitative,* but gradually the music became more important.

In the Beginning

Claudio Monteverdi (1567-1643) is considered to have been the first great composer of opera. The first English language opera was composed by Henry Purcell (1659-1695), who was appointed organist at Westminster Abbey in London, in 1679. Like Monteverdi, he wrote both religious pieces and *entertainments* (amusing pieces) for the king's court.

Big Daddy

Johann Sebastian Bach (1685-1750) is often regarded as the greatest composer of the Baroque Era. He not only produced a vast amount of music, particularly a lot of religious works, but he also had twenty children! Three of his sons became famous composers and musicians in their own right.

Johann Sebastian Bach

Crashing Chords

The piano was invented by an Italian called Bartolomeo Cristofori (1655-1731), in the early 1700s. He called his new instrument the pianoforte, which means 'soft-loud', because it could be played both very loudly and very quietly. Up until then, everyone had played on the harpsichord, which cannot change its volume.

Super Strads

The most outstanding violin maker, Antonio Stradivari (1644-1737), made over one thousand violins in his lifetime. Each one bears a special label, and nowadays they fetch such vast sums of money that only a very few players can ever afford to own one. At a sale in London, in November 1990, one of Stradivari's violins (known as a Stradivarius) was sold for £902,000.

Room Music

In contrast to the tremendous musical sounds of opera, another form of music developed at the same time. It was called *chamber music*, literally meaning 'room music'. Three or four instruments – usually two violins, a viola and a cello – have what is virtually a conversation with each other.

String quartet

CLASSICAL MUSIC 1750-1824

This period in the history of music was dominated by three big names: Haydn, Mozart and Beethoven. The musical style changed, with strong tunes taking the place of the intricate baroque style. More instruments were added to the standard collection of players and the modern symphony orchestra was born.

Haydn

The symphony as we know it today was perfected by Franz Joseph Haydn (1732-1809). Haydn was appointed music director to Prince Paul Esterházy, whose patronage (support) enabled the composer to devote all his energy to his music. It obviously worked, as Haydn composed one hundred and four symphonies in his lifetime!

Mozart

Wolfgang Amadeus Mozart (1756-1791) was a child prodigy (he was unusually talented), playing and composing his first *sonata* at the age of five and his first opera at twelve. In his short life he wrote some one thousand pieces of music, although only seventy of these were published in his lifetime. The enormous task of cataloguing his work was undertaken by an Austrian called Ludwig von Köchel, and every piece composed by Mozart has a 'K' number in its title. His great unfinished masterpiece the *Requiem,* for example, is K626.

Beethoven

Ludwig van Beethoven (1770-1827) is a towering figure in the world of music, linking the Classical and Romantic Eras.

He gradually lost his hearing, and this greatly affected his way of life. He would pound the piano so hard that the strings would break, and when he conducted the first performance of his ninth symphony (the *Choral Symphony*) he couldn't tell when the orchestra had finished playing or hear the audience's applause. However, he could still hear music in his head and so continued to compose, although he did become increasingly isolated from the world.

ROMANTIC MUSIC 1825-1874

After the seriousness of earlier music, composers of the Romantic Era began to 'paint pictures' and express emotions with their music, describing wild dreams or fantastic landscapes.

Seaside Music

If you listen to *Fingal's Cave* by the German composer Felix Mendelssohn (1809-1847), you can almost hear the waves crashing on the wild north coast of Scotland.

Singing Schubert Suppers

Franz Schubert (1797-1828) composed over six hundred songs called *lieder*. These songs were first sung at private parties for Schubert's friends, called *Schubertiads*. He made hardly any money from his compositions, yet today his music is sung all over the world.

Chopin

The Polish composer Frédéric Chopin (1810-1849) wrote almost all his music for the piano, and his virtuoso performances greatly increased public interest in the piano. Through his music, Chopin revealed his most intimate feelings, and was known as the 'poet of music'.

Mr and Mrs Schumann

Robert Schumann (1810-1856) was a German composer of songs and piano music. In 1840 he married Clara Wieck (1819-1896), who was an acclaimed pianist in her own right. Her father had long opposed their marriage, but she was obviously a great inspiration to Schumann, because after their wedding he produced a vast quantity of songs.

Magical Mythology

The longest opera cycle (a series of related works) ever is called *Der Ring des Nibelungen,* and it is made up of four operas. When played in full, it takes sixteen hours to perform!

Wagner took around twenty six years to compose the cycle, taking the stories of gods and goddesses, magic, hoards of gold, and giants and dragons from German mythology.

Tchaikovsky

Pyotr Ilyich Tchaikovsky (1840-1893) had a very sad life, but left behind some of the most popular classical music ever written.

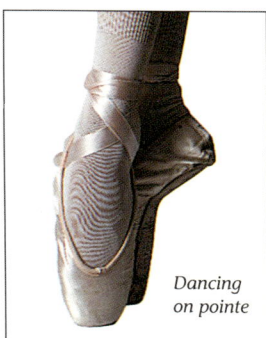

Dancing on pointe

He is best remembered for his ballets *The Nutcracker, Swan Lake* and *The Sleeping Beauty.* His *1812 Overture* contains cannon effects, and Tchaikovsky himself described it as 'very loud and noisy'.

NATIONAL MUSIC 1875-1899

Traditionally, classical music had been dominated by Italian, German and Austrian composers, but by the turn of the 19th century, composers from other European countries became better known.

Home Comforts

Georges Bizet (1838-1875) from France, Edvard Grieg (1843-1907) from Norway, Bedřich Smetana (1824-1884) from Czechoslovakia and Edward Elgar (1857-1934) from England all composed music that reflected their homelands.

Bizet

Gypsy Girl

Audiences were shocked when they heard Georges Bizet's opera *Carmen*. It is a hot-blooded and tragic story of a gypsy girl who worked in a cigarette factory. Bizet died just three months after the first performance, so he never knew the success of *Carmen*, which is now probably the most popular opera of all time.

Stars and Stripes

Antonín Dvořák (1841-1904) moved from his home in Czechoslovakia to the United States, where he composed his famous ninth symphony, *From The New World* (otherwise known as the *New World Symphony*). It was inspired partly by Black American folk music.

Standing Room Only

Gustav Mahler (1860-1911) wrote ten huge symphonies. The eighth is known as the *Symphony of a Thousand* because it requires an enormous orchestra of over one hundred players, eight solo singers, a double chorus and a boy's chorus to perform it. There were actually more than one thousand players and performers on stage at the first performance in Munich, in 1910, with Mahler himself conducting.

Musical Bambi

In 1894, the French composer Claude Debussy (1862-1918) wrote a piece called *Prélude à l'Après-midi d'un Faune,* meaning the afternoon of a fawn (young deer). This marked the beginning of what is called *impressionist* music. The music conveys the thoughts of a fawn as it lies dozing in a shady wood in the heat of a summer afternoon.

REVOLUTIONARY AND MODER[N]

With the dawning of the new century, some composers began to look at new ways of creating exciting music.

The Shock of the New

In 1912, *Pierrot Lunaire,* by Arnold Schoenberg (1874-1951), had its premiere. One critic wrote, "If this is music then I pray my Creator not to let me hear it again." It is a setting of poems full of references to blood, corpses and skulls!

What a Riot!

At the first performance of the ballet *The Rite of Spring* by Igor Stravinsky (1882-1971), in Paris, 1913, the audience rioted. They were making so much noise that they even managed to drown out the music!

Musical Nonsense

The French composer Erik Satie (1866-1925) wrote some very simple and beautiful music, but he also had a great sense of humour and poked fun at those who were too serious about music. Two of his pieces are called *Tunes to Make You Run Away* and *Pieces in the Shape of a Pear.*

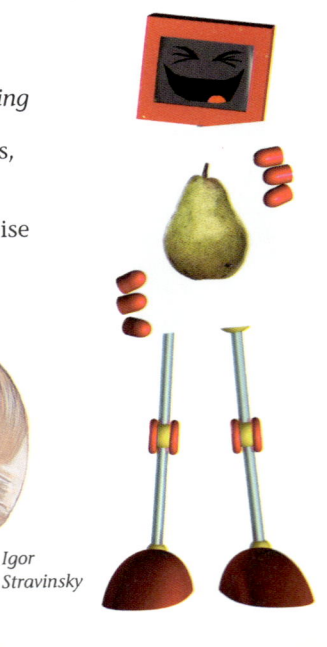

Igor Stravinsky

Going on Record

Music had been recorded in many strange ways until 1925, when the electrical process arrived and the quality of reproduction improved overnight. The first ever electrical recording was of Tchaikovsky's fourth symphony.

Please Yourself

Composers began to leave more to chance, and a new style of music developed called *random music*. Performers could decide what to play from the composer's slightest guidelines. John Cage (1912-1992) actually wrote a piece of four minutes and thirty three seconds of absolute silence.

Grand piano

Musical Machines

The invention of the computer and the synthesizer has dramatically extended the range of sounds and noises that a composer can use when writing. Ordinary sounds can be speeded up or slowed down, played backwards or over and over again, and reassembled in endless variations.

WORLDWIDE MUSIC

All over the world, people listen to and play music. There are an enormous number of different styles of playing, and thousands and thousands of different instruments. Music is part of everyday life, from religious worship to entertainment.

Boom, Boom

The Bedouin (nomadic) tribesmen in the Sahara Desert base the rhythms of their music and songs on the steady tread of the camel's feet as they plod over the sand.

Stick Your Tongue Out

In New Zealand, Maori warriors perform a war dance called a *haka*. Adopted by New Zealand rugby players, the dance involves shouting, foot stamping and the pulling of faces.

Drumming Feet

In Africa, drums are often carved into the shape of human legs, with two feet to stand on. They are used to send messages, as well as providing the music for tribal dancing.

New Zealand rugby players warming up for a game.

Real Horns

The shofar, an instrument made from a ram's horn, is mentioned in the Bible and is still used in Hebrew religious ceremonies.

Tunes of the Gods

Panpipes were played as early as 200 BC and they can still be heard today in Bolivia, Peru and other parts of South America. The pipes are made of bamboo and get their name from the Greek god Pan.

Panpipes

Drums, Gongs and Bells

The music of China and Japan has very ancient origins. Most of it was composed for performance at court, but music also played a very important part in the Buddhist and Shinto temples. Much of the music is played on percussion instruments, such as drums, gongs, cymbals and bells.

Chinese chimes

Ragas

Indian classical music is based on a very complicated series of scales known as *ragas*. There are special ragas for different times of day and seasons of the year. They are usually played on a stringed instrument called a sitar.

Sitar

THE HUMAN VOICE

The most versatile instrument of all is the human voice. Just think of all the different styles of singing – from pop and rock to grand opera.

Call to Prayer

In Islamic countries, a muezzin, or crier, calls people to prayer several times during the day from a minaret (tower) on top of a mosque. The prophet Mohammed decreed that music could only be used for this purpose, or alongside readings from the Koran.

Dream Time

In Australia, Aborigines recount the history of their culture and beliefs with singing and hand clapping. Many of their songs tell how the earth was created.

Boys Only

The tradition of having boy sopranos or trebles dates from the Middle Ages, when women were forbidden to sing in church. Nowadays, however, many of the great cathedrals have girls' choirs as well.

It's All in the Technique

Pop singers use microphones to project their voices, while opera singers have to 'throw' their voices without any electronic help. Their singing techniques are very different, as are the sounds that they make.

Full of Puff

The bass singer Luigi Lablache (1794-1858), who taught Queen Victoria to sing, must have had pretty amazing lungs. He could sing a long note from soft to loud and back to soft again, drink a glass of wine, sing a twelve-note scale while trilling on each note and blow out a candle with his mouth open – all in one breath!

Opera Singers Go Pop!

Placido Domingo, Luciano Pavarotti and José Carreras – known as 'The Three Tenors' – joined forces to perform a truly remarkable concert in Rome, in 1990. The recording of the event shot the three singers into the superstar league of the pop charts, selling millions of copies.

What is an orchestra?

An orchestra is a large group of musicians who play a wide variety of instruments together. 'Orchestra' comes from the Greek name for the semicircular space in front of a stage.

World Famous

There are now large symphony orchestras in most of the world's big cities. They go on tour regularly, so it's possible to hear wonderful music from a wide variety of players. The first modern symphony orchestra was founded in Mannheim, Germany, in 1743.

Still Playing...

The oldest surviving symphony orchestra is the Gewandhaus Orchestra of Leipzig, Germany. It began playing in 1743, in a specially built concert hall paid for by the city's linen merchants.

Ancient Beginnings

A gamelan is a type of orchestra found in Indonesia. It is composed mainly of percussion instruments, such as gongs and *metallophones* (instruments with tuned metal bars which are struck with a hammer, such as a glockenspiel). According to legend, the first gamelan players were the ancient gods, who 'spoke' to each other with gongs and chimes.

Raising Money

It takes a huge amount of time, effort and money to run a major orchestra. Some of this money can be generated by concert ticket sales, but nowadays recording contracts are probably more important. If people can't make it to a concert, they can buy compact discs, tapes or long playing records, featuring the music of their favourite orchestras.

A Way of Life

Playing in one of the leading orchestras is a bit like living in a great big family. It is very hard work, though, with lots of rehearsals and travelling, and the players need to be of the highest standard to gain and keep their places.

WHERE THEY ALL SIT

The modern orchestra is divided into four main groups of instruments: strings, woodwind, brass and percussion. The players sit in a semicircle facing the conductor. The strings are at the front; behind them comes the woodwind section in the centre; the brass and percussion instruments are arranged along the back of the orchestra.

Soaring Strings

The string section is usually the largest section in an orchestra. It is made up of first and second violins, violas, cellos and double basses – all members of the violin family. The violin is the smallest in the family, played tucked under the chin, while the huge double bass stands at an awesome 1.8 m (6 ft).

Wonderful Woodwind

The extremely varied woodwind section usually consists of one piccolo, two flutes, two oboes, two clarinets, one bass clarinet, one cor anglais, two bassoons and one double bassoon.

Blazing Brass

The brass instruments are among the loudest in the orchestra. The average orchestra has three trumpets, four French horns, three trombones and a tuba. Brass players need to do lots of breathing exercises, so that they don't run out of puff at a crucial moment!

Pounding Percussion

The array of instruments a percussionist can be asked to play is almost endless. Some of the instruments are very familiar – such as cymbals, the tiny triangle and the xylophone – but others sound really weird – such as blocks, tubular bells, claves, the flexatone and the thunder sheet!

Best known are the drums, ranging from the precise ratatat of the side drum, to the deep boom of the bass drum.

THE CONDUCTOR

In the early days there were no conductors; a harpsichord player would keep time. But as music became more complex, a conductor became more necessary.

Scoring Points

The conductor must know the *score* of the music inside out. It is the conductor's responsibility to explain to the players how the piece must be played technically, and how the composer's wishes should be interpreted.

Baton Behaviour

Conductors use either a long or short baton, while others just use their hands. Generally, the right hand indicates the speed at which the orchestra should be playing, while the left is used to interpret the piece.

A Couple of the Famous

Leopold Stokowski (1882-1977) conducted an orchestra for the first time when he was only twelve years old, and continued right up to the day he died.

Arturo Toscanini (1867-1957) seemed to have an almost hypnotic power over the orchestras he conducted.

Andrew Davis

THE COMPOSER

All music has been created by someone. A composer writes music in the same way that an author writes a book or an artist paints a picture. It is a combination of natural talent and study.

Inspiration

The sound of the wind, reading a poem – any thing can inspire the composer to write a piece of music.

In Their Own Words

"About a third of our songs are pure slog." (Paul McCartney)

"...the fruits of long and laborious endeavour." (Mozart)

"All the inspiration I ever needed was a phonecall from a producer." (Cole Porter)

Especially For You

Composers are often asked to write special pieces of music, to commemorate important events. One such event was the tragic death of Princess Diana in August, 1997. Elton John dedicated the rewritten version of his single *Candle in the Wind* to her, and all the funds went to charity. It became the biggest selling single by a UK artist of all time.

Movie Music

Music that is written for film and television adds to what is being seen on screen. The composer works closely with the film producer.

THE PLAYERS

Musicians can be soloists, part of a small group such as a string quartet, or one of a huge team such as an orchestra. Usually, they specialise in playing just one or two instruments, unless they play percussion.

The International Stage

The famous musicians of today come from all over the world. Mitsuko Uchida (1948-), renowned for her piano playing of Mozart, is from Japan; Wynton Marsalis (1961-), a jazz and classical trumpet player, is from America; and Marisa Robles (1937-), a harpist who has written music based on the Narnia books by C. S. Lewis, is from Spain.

Wynton Marsalis

Fully Fit

Musicians need to be fit to cope with all the stresses and strains of their hectic lives. Woodwind and brass players need plenty of puff, string players need nimble fingers and percussionists need to be physically strong, to beat those drums!

Youngest and Oldest

Mozart gave his first public performance on the violin at the age of six. The Romanian pianist Cella Delavrancea gave her last performance at the age of one hundred and three!

Am I Too Loud?

A player who is often overlooked is the accompanist – the person who plays an instrument, often the piano, to support another player. One of the most famous was Gerald Moore (1899-1986), who played with many of the greatest singers and instrumentalists in the world.

WEIRD AND WONDERFUL

Some of the earliest instruments had very strange names, such as the serpent, gittern, shawm, tabor, racket and flageolet. Some equally strange ones are still being played today.

The bull-roarer is made of a piece of wood attached to a length of cord which is spun through the air to make a roaring sound.

The didgeridoo is made of a hollowed-out bamboo pipe and makes a booming sound. Traditionally, only men are allowed to play this sacred Aboriginal instrument.

The tiktiri is a kind of double clarinet used by Indian snake charmers.

The shamisen is a kind of lute played in Japan as an accompaniment to traditional plays. It has three strings which are tuned according to the mood of the play.

Shamisen

The bosun's whistle is still used today to pipe senior naval officers on board ship.

Traditionally, the West Indian steel drum is made from an oil drum. Instead of a skin covering, it has a curved metal dish of various panels (right). These sound different notes when hit.

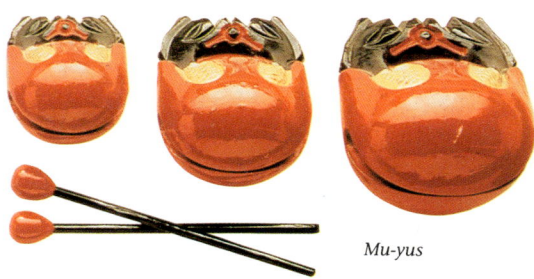

Mu-yus

Mu-yus, or temple blocks, originated in China and are carved to resemble fish.

The urua is a type of huge double clarinet measuring several feet long. It is played by Brazilian Indians.

Early 1900s Hungarian bagpipes

Although we tend to associate the bagpipes with Scotland, they were around as early as Roman times. They are still played in many parts of the world today, in some shape or another.

MAKING INSTRUMENTS

The earliest instruments were simple bones, shells or reeds that produced a sound when blown into. Nowadays, instrument making is highly skilled and is mainly done by hand, just as it has been for centuries.

Timeless Craft

Antonio Stradivari's original instructions on the making of the violin have changed very little since 1700. A violin is made of several different kinds of wood – maple, pine, spruce, ebony and rosewood being a few of the choices.

Brass Tacks

Horns were originally made of animal horns, hence the name. The brass instruments that we use today are made in several different sections. There is often an amazing length of metal coiled up in the finished instrument. The biggest tuba, which is 2.4 m (8 ft) tall, would measure nearly 14 m (45 ft) long if all its pipe work was stretched out!

Violin

East African horn made from gazelle horn

French horn

Tuba

Terrific Timpani

Kettledrums, or timpani, were originally carried on camel or horseback by Turkish soldiers, and were brought back to Europe by the Crusaders. Modern timpani is made by stretching a piece of calfskin tightly over a huge copper bowl.

Kettledrums (timpani)

Taking the Strain

The strings of an upright piano are stretched over a cast-iron frame capable of taking a strain of up to 17 tonnes! The keys have been arranged in the same order since the days of the early keyboard.

Revived Recorders

The recorder was a very popular instrument in the 1500s and 1600s, but then it was almost forgotten about until the early 1900s.

After losing his own recorder, Arnold Dolmetsch (1858-1940) decided to make a new instrument based on the design of the original, and the present-day instrument was born!

Descant recorder

THE ELECTRONIC REVOLUTION

In the future we might well sit in a concert hall just looking at banks of machinery as computers 'play' for us. Although the computer could not be called a musical instrument, its introduction to the world of sound has produced some impressive results.

All In One

In the early 1960s, an American engineer called Robert Moog (1934-) developed the first synthesizer. A synthesizer can reproduce the sound of any instrument or actually create new ones – it has completely revolutionised electronic music.

One-man Band

With the use of computers, it is now possible for one player, sitting in front of a console, to produce a sound that would conventionally take hundreds of players and support staff to produce.

Synthesizer player

Synthesizer keyboard – controls can create new sounds and store them

Playing at Home

Music software on small discs can now be fed into the ordinary home computer to produce musical sounds and even create compositions. It can correct mistakes and adjust the tempo of the playing. A piece of equipment called an expander can be linked to the computer or to an electronic instrument to extend the range of sounds produced.

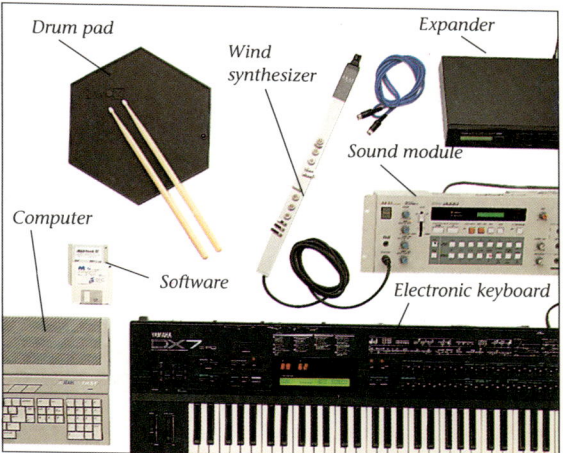

Musician or Technician?

Musicians who use electronic equipment have to travel with vast numbers of technicians to connect, maintain and repair it. In live performances, these technicians are every bit as important as the superstars who are at the front of the stage.

Composers Too

Modern classical music has been greatly influenced by technology. Composers are no longer confined to conventional sounds. They have such a variety of effects at their fingertips that it is reflected in their compositions.

ROCK AND POP MUSIC

There has been popular music since the street ballads sung by the wandering minstrels in the Middle Ages, but *pop* as we know it probably dates from the early 1950s, when music first began to speak directly to young people.

The King

Elvis Presley (1935-1977) had his first hit with *Heartbreak Hotel* in 1956, and he went on to become a rock-and-roll superstar. To date, he has had more albums in the charts than any other solo singer. When he died, his estate was presented with 50 platinum discs and 60 gold discs – a world record.

The Fab Four

The Beatles had their first UK hit with *Love Me Do*, in 1962. The combination of good rock-and-roll playing and excellent songwriting by John Lennon and Paul McCartney had a huge influence on the world of pop music. To date, the world-wide sales of their hit *I Want to Hold Your Hand* exceed 12 million copies.

The Beatles

Heavy Metal

After The Beatles and The Rolling Stones came loud, aggressive music. It was given the name *heavy metal*. At the same time, America was producing a combination of gospel music and rhythm and blues – it became known as *soul*. In the late 1970s, the wildest forms of rock and roll became known as *punk rock*.

Mega Success

The 1980s and 1990s saw the rise of pop superstars such as Michael Jackson and Madonna, whose recordings sell millions of copies and who can fill huge stadiums at live concerts.

Here Today, Gone Tomorrow

Modern groups come and go as fast as they are formed. Some of this year's hits will be completely forgotten by next year.

New Relationships

Pop and classical music are no longer at opposite ends of the music scale. Groups who play violins and cellos are now just as likely to incorporate electric guitars into their music.

JAZZ

Jazz music has its origins in New Orleans, USA, in the late 1890s. It is a combination of African rhythms and Black American *improvisation* (playing without previous planning). The earliest jazz was vocal music, and this extended into the three instrument line-up of trumpet, trombone and clarinet.

Satchmo

Louis Armstrong (1901-1971) was a brilliant brass player who achieved world-wide recognition for his trumpet and cornet playing. He was given his nickname 'Satchmo' because he had a very wide mouth that looked like a satchel!

The Empress of the Blues

Bessie Smith (1894-1937), who was known as 'The Empress of the Blues', made her singing debut in 1903, aged nine. One of the earliest jazz singers, she sang twelve-bar blues songs about the hardships of life and the poverty that many of her fellow Black Americans endured.

Louis Armstrong

The Duke

Edward Kennedy Ellington (1899-1974), known as 'Duke Ellington', was another huge figure in the growth of jazz. He was a pianist who went on to lead one of the most influential jazz bands ever. One of his pieces, *Such Sweet Thunder,* is a dedication to Shakespeare, and is jazz mixed with classical music.

Duke Ellington

In the Mood

In the 1930s, trombonist Glenn Miller (1904-1944) and his dance band brought a new style of jazz called *swing* to an even wider audience. In 1944, the plane in which Glenn Miller was travelling mysteriously disappeared over the English Channel. He was never seen again.

Jazz Today

Today, jazz is a mixture of modern and traditional playing. As with other forms of music, there is a merging of pop, classical music and jazz. One best-selling recording is a blend of the earliest plainsong (unaccompanied vocal music) performed by four male voices, and the very modern sounds of the saxophone.

THE SOUND OF MUSIC

Thomas Edison made the first sound recording on his phonograph, in 1877, and Émile Berliner made the first flat disc record player, or gramophone, in 1888. With the development of the radio valve, in 1906, broadcasting became a real possibility, and by the 1920s most places had their own radio stations. Suddenly there was a huge audience for music.

Long Players

In 1948, long-playing vinyl records appeared, quickly taking the place of the old shellac (resin) discs. The new LPs could store much more sound on them, and the quality of reproduction was also better.

From LP to CD

In the 1980s, digital technology vastly improved sound recording. Compact discs are metallic engraved discs that are read by a laser beam. They are easy to carry around and you can listen to them practically anywhere.

An early record player – the gramophone

Music Over the Globe

The Live Aid concert in 1985 was shown around the world as it took place by the use of communication satellites. Once upon a time, this kind of broadcast would have required a chain of transmitters, but the signal was simply beamed up to the satellite.

Built For Music

Originally, music was heard in small private rooms at court or in church, but as the demand for public music grew, concert halls were built. Nowadays, the acoustic (sound) demands of public buildings are huge, as they must be able to take the biggest pop concert or the smallest string quartet recital.

Sydney Opera House

STRANGE BUT TRUE

The French composer Jean Baptiste Lully (1632-1687) crushed his toe with a wooden staff while beating time with it on the floor. He died of gangrene shortly afterwards.

The biggest ever grand piano weighed 1.25 tonnes and was 3.55 m (11 1/2 ft) long.

The organ in an auditorium in New Jersey, America, can make as much noise as 25 brass bands.

In 1991, the opera singer Placido Domingo was applauded for one hour and twenty minutes after a performance of *Otello*.

If you were to straighten out a French horn it would measure 9 m (30 ft) long.

The longest symphony ever written was by Richard Rodgers (1902-1979) and lasts 13 hours. Not surprisingly, it isn't played too often!

About 42,000 operas have been written since Monteverdi wrote the first in 1607.

The largest orchestra ever performed in Boston, USA, in 1872. It consisted of almost 1,000 players, including 400 first violins.

All the instruments in an orchestra are tuned to the oboe, as it stays in tune the best.

Mozart is alleged to have played billiards while he was composing.

John Philip Sousa (1854-1932) invented a giant brass instrument known as the sousaphone. It is over 2 m (7 ft) in height.

Until 1970, there was a law in Oman, in the Middle East, making it illegal to play the drums.

Some pipes and flutes can be played with the nose as well as the mouth.

The virtuoso Italian violinist Niccolò Paganini (1782-1840) could play so incredibly fast that people said he must be in league with the devil.

Handel's *Music for the Royal Fireworks* was actually written to accompany a firework display in London in 1749.

An instrument called the serpent was invented in France, in 1590. It was over 2 m (6 1/2 ft) long and bent into an 's' shape. It has now been replaced by the tuba.

Camille Saint-Saëns (1835-1921) used the xylophone in his composition *Danse Macabre* to make the sound of skeletons dancing.

By the age of five, Handel could play the harpsichord, organ, violin and oboe!

The Bach family produced at least 76 musicians, and more than 50 of the Bachs had the same first name – Johann.

Haydn's string quartet in E flat is called *The Joke*, because the last movement keeps stopping and starting, so the audience doesn't know when the piece has finished.

Thomas Alva Edison (1847-1931), who invented the phonograph, originally intended it to be used as a dictating machine in the office.

41

A TO Z OF COMPOSERS

Bach, Johann Sebastian, (1685-1750), German. Often regarded as greatest composer of Baroque Era. Central figure in development of Western classical music and renowned keyboard player.

Bartók, Béla, (1881-1945), Hungarian. Composer of ballet *The Miraculous Mandarin*. He wrote graded pieces for piano.

Beethoven, Ludwig van, (1770-1827), German. Dominant influence on 19th century music. His third, fifth, sixth and ninth symphonies are his most famous. He composed after going deaf.

Berlioz, Hector, (1803-1869), French. Had to earn living as critic, despite writing some of the most romantic music ever. Considered as founder of modern orchestration.

Bizet, Georges, (1838-1875), French. Composer of famous *Toreador's Song* from his opera *Carmen*.

Brahms, Johannes, (1833-1897), German. He used to play piano in inns and dance halls to earn money. One of greatest composers of symphonic music and songs.

Britten, Benjamin, (1913-1976), English. Composer of several great operas including *Peter Grimes*. Wrote special pieces for children such as *The Young Person's Guide to the Orchestra*.

Cage, John, (1912-1992), American. Experimental composer whose ideas included using radio static and placing pieces of paper around piano strings to distort the sound.

Chopin, Frédéric, (1810-1849), Polish. One of the greatest pianists, but performed publicly only 30 times.

Debussy, Claude, (1862-1918), French. Pioneer of impressionist music.

Dvořák, Antonín, (1841-1904), Czechoslovakian. Was a butcher's boy before studying music. Composed *From The New World*.

Elgar, Edward, (1857-1934), English. Wrote popular and moving *Enigma Variations*. One of first composers to make gramophone recordings.

Fauré, Gabriel, (1845-1924), French. Was a church musician but is most remembered for his *Requiem*.

Gershwin, George, (1898-1937), American. Composed *Porgy and Bess*, incorporating jazz rhythms and popular song styles in an operatic format.

Grieg, Edvard, (1843-1907), Norwegian. Nationalist composer best known for *Peer Gynt* – his music for the play by Norwegian playwright Henrik Ibsen.

Handel, George Frederick, (1685-1759), German. His massive oratorio, the *Messiah,* was written in just three weeks. It contains the famous *Hallelujah Chorus*.

Haydn, Franz Joseph, (1732-1809), Austrian. Known as 'the father of the symphony'. Taught Beethoven and was friends with Mozart. First great master of the string quartet.

Liszt, Franz, (1811-1886), Hungarian. Virtuoso of piano and established concert artist by age of 12. Produced an opera at the age of 14. Some of his piano compositions are considered to be the most difficult ever written.

Mahler, Gustav, (1860-1911), Austrian. Composer of very romantic music, especially fifth symphony.

Mendelssohn, Felix, (1809-1847), German. Composer of *Wedding March,* often played at marriage ceremonies.

Monteverdi, Claudio, (1567-1643), Italian. Wrote first major operas, but only three complete ones survive.

Mozart, Wolfgang Amadeus, (1756-1791), Austrian. Died penniless before world acknowledged his greatness. Works include *The Marriage of Figaro* and *The Magic Flute. Requiem* finished by pupil after death.

Offenbach, Jacques, (1819-1880), German. Born in Germany, but regarded as French composer. Wrote around one hundred operettas. Remembered for his *Barcarolle* and *Orpheus in the Underworld*

Purcell, Henry, (1659-1695), English. Wrote ceremonial music for courts of James II then William and Mary. Also wrote for theatre and church.

Rachmaninov, Sergei, (1873-1943), Russian. Best known for piano concertos. Left Russia in 1917 and made his home in United States.

Rimsky-Korsakov, Nikolai, (1844-1908), Russian. Composer of famous *Flight of the Bumble Bee.*

Rossini, Gioacchino, (1792-1868), Italian. Wrote thirty six operas in nineteen years, then stopped composing for ever. Composed operas *The Barber of Seville* and *William Tell.*

Satie, Erik, (1866-1925), French. Wrote mainly short and simple pieces such as *Three Gymnopédies.* He is known for his humorous music.

Schoenberg, Arnold, (1874-1951), Austrian. Developed twelve-note or serial music. Had a huge influence on modern music.

Schubert, Franz, (1797-1828), Austrian. Slept with glasses on in case he had song idea at night and needed to write it down. Wrote over 600 songs.

Schumann, Robert, (1810-1856), German. Best remembered for piano music including *Scenes from Childhood*.

Shostakovich, Dmitri, (1906-1975), Russian. Wrote his heroic *Leningrad Symphony* during siege of Leningrad by Germans in World War II.

Sibelius, Jean, (1865-1957), Finnish. Best remembered for his music based on Finnish mythology such as *Finlandia*.

Strauss, Johann II, (1825-1899), Austrian. 'Waltz king' of Vienna. Famous for *The Blue Danube* and *Die Fledermaus*.

Stravinsky, Igor, (1882-1971), Russian. Best known for ballet music *The Firebird, Petrushka* and *The Rite of Spring*.

Tchaikovsky, Pyotr Ilyich, (1840-1893), Russian. Highly tuneful music includes six symphonies, three piano concertos and ballets – *Swan Lake, The Sleeping Beauty* and *The Nutcracker*.

Verdi, Giuseppe, (1813-1901), Italian. Most successful opera composer of his generation. Of 27 operas, most famous are *La Traviata, Aida* and *Rigoletto*.

Vivaldi, Antonio, (1678-1741), Italian. Violinist and composer, he died in poverty. Work largely neglected until *The Four Seasons* became popular in 1800s.

Wagner, Richard, (1813-1883), German. Towering opera composer whose works include *Der Ring des Nibelungen* and *Tristan and Isolde*.

A TO Z OF MUSICAL TERMS

Accompaniment A musical instrument or piece of music that is played to support the main musician.

Aria A vocal piece for a singer, usually found in operas.

Baritone The adult male voice which is lower than a tenor but higher than a bass.

Bass The lowest male voice.

Beat A unit of time used in music.

Chamber Music Music performed by a small group of musicians.

Chord Two or more notes that are all played at the same time.

Concerto A piece of music for an orchestra or one or more soloists.

Conductor A person who directs a group of players or singers.

Contralto The lowest female voice.

Descant The part sung by the highest voices.

Duet A piece for two players.

Harmony A pleasant musical sound or a tune that blends with the main melody.

Libretto The words of an opera, like the script of a play.

Melody A series of notes played one after another to form a tune.

Motet A short choral piece, usually sung unaccompanied.

Movement A section in a piece of music.

Notation The way music is written down, usually on a staff.

Opera A play where the story is told through singing and acting.

Operetta A comic or light-hearted opera.

Oratorio A large scale religious work which is written for soloists, a chorus and an orchestra.

Quartet Four voices or instruments singing or playing together.

Requiem A piece of music performed as a remembrance of someone who has died.

Rhythm The lengths of the notes in a piece of music. Music mostly has rhythms with notes of different lengths, which come in repeated patterns.

Scale A series of notes played one after the other, from the lowest to the highest or vice versa.

Score A copy of a piece of music in which all the different players' parts are shown.

Solo A piece of music for a single voice or instrument.

Sonata A piece of music often with three or four movements. For piano alone, or for any other instrument, usually with piano accompaniment.

Soprano The highest female voice.

Staff (or stave) The set of five lines on which musical notes are placed.

Symphony A large-scale composition for an orchestra, usually consisting of four separate movements.

Tempo The speed of a piece of music.

Tenor The adult male voice, higher than a baritone or a bass.

Treble A boy with the same vocal range as a soprano.

Virtuoso An outstandingly good singer or performer who can play the most difficult music.

INDEX

accompanist 27
Ancient Egyptians 2
Ancient Greeks 3

ballet 11, 42, 45
Baroque Era 6-7, 8, 42

CDs 21, 38
chamber music 7, 46
choirs 5, 18
Classical Era 8-9
composers 4, 5, 6, 8, 9, 10, 11, 12, 13, 14, 15, 24, 25, 33, 40, 42-45
computers 15, 32-33
concerts 19, 20, 21, 32, 35, 39, 43
conductors 22, 24, 46

impressionist music 13, 43
instruments
 brass
  French horn 23, 30, 40
  trombone 23, 36, 37
  trumpet 3, 23, 26, 36
  tuba 23, 30
 early 2-3, 16-17, 28-31
 electronic 15, 19, 32-33, 35, 38
 keyboard
  harpsichord 7, 24, 41
  piano 7, 9, 10, 11, 15, 26, 27, 31, 37, 40, 42, 43, 44, 45, 47
 percussion
  cymbals 17, 23
  drums 16, 17, 23, 26, 29, 33, 41
  glockenspiel 21
  triangle 23
  xylophone 23, 41
 stringed
  cello 7, 22, 35
  double bass 22
  guitar 35
  harp 2, 26
  viola 7, 22
  violin 7, 22, 27, 30, 35, 41
 unusual 28-29
 wind
  bassoon 22
  clarinet 22, 29, 36
  cor anglais 22
  flute 22, 41
  oboe 22, 40, 41
  panpipes 17
  piccolo 22
  recorder 31
  saxophone 37

jazz 36-37

keyboard 31-33

LPs 21, 38

Middle Ages 4-5, 18, 34
musical terms 46-47

opera 6, 7, 9, 11, 12, 18, 19, 40, 42, 44, 45, 46, 47
orchestra 3, 8, 9, 13, 20-23, 24, 26, 40, 42

popular (pop) music 5, 18, 19, 34-35, 37, 39

religious music 2, 4, 5, 6, 16, 17, 18, 47
rock music 18, 34-35
Romans 3
Romantic Era 10-11, 42, 44

singing 2, 4, 5, 6, 13, 18-19, 34-35, 36, 46, 47
synthesizer 15, 32

troubadours 4

48